VIETNAM WAR VETERAN
Memoir

MODERN
DAILY PRESS

Vietnam War Veterans Memoir

Copyright © 2025
by Modern Daily Press

All rights reserved. No part of this publication may be reproduced, stored or transmitted in any form or by any means, electronic, mechanical, photocopying, recording, scanning, or otherwise without written permission from the publisher. It is illegal to copy this book, post it to a website, or distribute it by any other means without permission.

Disclaimers and Terms of Use: The publisher and author do not warrant or represent that the contents within are accurate and disclaim all warranties and is not liable for any damages whatsoever. The information provided herein does not, and is not intended to, constitute legal nor professional advice; instead, all information, content, and materials available are for general informational purposes only. Readers should contact their attorney to obtain advice with respect to any particular legal matter. No reader of this publication should act or refrain from acting on the basis of information on this publication without first seeking legal advice from counsel in the relevant jurisdiction. Although all attempts were made to verify information, they do not assume any responsibility for errors, omissions, or contrary interpretation of the subject matter contained within as perceived slights of peoples, persons, organizations are unintentional and information contained within should not be used as a source of legal, business, accounting, financial, or other professional advice. Publisher and author has no responsibility for the persistence or accuracy of URLs for external or third-party Internet Websites referred to in this publication and does not guarantee that any content on such Websites is, or will remain, accurate or appropriate.

Product names, logos, brands, and other trademarks featured or referred to within this publication are the property of their respective trademark holders and are not sponsored, approved, licensed, or endorsed by any of their licensees or affiliates. Some images shown may be generated using artificial intelligence and should not be considered real photographs or accurate representations of actual events or persons.

BONUS DOWNLOADS INCLUDED

Download 3 Free Books As Our Bonus Content

What You'll Get:

Scan Here for Bonus Downloads

No Purchase • Instant Access • Safe Download

Dedication

This book is dedicated to the bravest men and women who fought during the Vietnam War, who served in battle, and those who helped on the home front. Never to be forgotten, your sacrifice, courage, and resilience will inspire generations to come to uphold the principles of service, perseverance, and compassion.

CONTENT

Opening 9

PART ONE: HEROES IN BATTLE

An American Green Beret 15

Naval Aviator Turned Prisoner of War 23

The African American Medic Hero 31

The Grunt Padre 39

Best General in The South Vietnamese Army 47

PART TWO: HUMANITARIAN HEROES

Civilian Warrior 57

Orphanage in Saigon 63

Soldier-Scholar 69

Founder of The School of Youth for Social Service 75

Red Cross Volunteers 81

PART THREE: NOTABLE INDIVIDUALS

Commander of The U.S Forces in Vietnam 87

Breaker of The Pentagon Papers 93

About Us 105

OPENING

When I began writing this book, I was constantly amazed by the resilience, courage, and sacrifices of the individuals whose stories fill these pages. Their lives, choices, and defining moments are more than historical accounts; they are lessons in bravery, perseverance, and the human spirit. The events may have happened years ago, but their significance remains as powerful today. The people I will discuss in this book made choices that changed the world around them. Their stories should not fade with time. Instead, they should be passed down and honored, and never forgotten.

This book is divided into three parts, each highlighting different aspects of heroism.

Part One: Heroes in Battle introduces you to extraordinary individuals who displayed unmatched bravery in combat. You'll learn about Roy Benavidez, a soldier who, despite being gravely wounded, refused to leave his fellow men behind. You'll read about Admiral James B. Stockdale, a prisoner of war who withstood unthinkable torture but never surrendered his dignity. You will also meet Lawrence Joel, a medic who risked his life to save others while under enemy fire, and Vincent R. Capodanno, a priest who gave his life offering comfort to soldiers in his final moments. These individuals remind us that courage is not just about fighting—it's about standing strong for others, even in the face of overwhelming odds.

Part Two: Humanitarian Heroes; the focus shifts to those who saved lives off the battlefield. War is not only fought with weapons but also through compassion, resilience, and the will to help others. You'll learn about Colonel Maggie, a woman who went from being an entertainer to a nurse, tending to wounded soldiers and civilians alike. You will also get to know about Sister Mary Laurence, a nun who devoted herself to protecting and caring for the children affected by the war. You'll explore the story of Bernard Fall, a journalist who risked everything to expose the realities of the Vietnam War. Additionally, you will get to learn about Thich Nhat Hanh, a Buddhist monk who dedicated his life to promoting peace and nonviolence. Finally, you will get to familiarize yourself with the "Donut Dollies," a group of women who volunteered to uplift soldiers' spirits, reminding them that they were not forgotten. These stories show that heroism isn't limited to the battlefield; it can be found in kindness, healing, and the simple act of giving hope.

Part Three: Notable Individuals highlights two pivotal figures shaping how the Vietnam War is remembered. General William Westmoreland, the military leader who commanded U.S. Forces in Vietnam, was responsible for critical decisions influencing the war's outcome. On the other side of history, journalist Neil Sheehan uncovered hidden truths through the Pentagon Papers, changing public perception of the war forever. Though on different sides of the war's narrative, these individuals undeniably made an impact on history.

By the time you finish reading this book, I hope you will see history not as a collection of dates and events but as a tapestry woven from the lives of real people who made difficult choices, who sacrificed for something greater than themselves, and who, in the process, defined what it means to be a hero. Heroism comes in many forms, and as you turn the pages, I invite you to reflect on how courage, kindness, and conviction can shape the world.

Let's begin with the first chapter: **"Heroes in Battle."**

PART ONE

HEROES IN BATTLE

1

AN AMERICAN GREEN BERET

MSG ROY P. BENAVIDEZ, THE ONE WHO SAVED HIS

FELLOW MEN WHILE BEING WOUNDED HIMSELF

BEFORE ENTERING THE WAR:

Being a child of non-American descent, Roy had a rough childhood. Born in the 1930s, he faced significant challenges as a non-American in the United States, particularly living in Texas, known for its conservative values.

He was constantly getting into fights because of racial discrimination. When his father passed away, they moved to Cuero, Texas, with his brother Rogelio and his mother. However, his mother passed away as well, due to tuberculosis.

With his parents gone, Roy and his brother moved to El Campo, Texas, to live with their Uncle Nicholas, Aunt Alexandria and Grandfather Salvador. So, even with his parents gone, he was still surrounded by family who cared for him like their own. However, Roy still faced difficulties as he was constantly subjected to racial slurs from the other kids. One kid even called him "pepper belly", which forced him into a fight that caught the attention of local police.

Because of all the fights, Roy dropped out of school at the age of fifteen. Accordingly, he also started to find work to provide for his family. His first job was with Art Haddock, a bookkeeper at a local Firestone. Haddock taught Roy many lessons in life, including responsibility. One of the rare things that Haddock did was treat Roy like a man, and with no discrimination whatsoever.

As grateful as Roy was for his job, he wanted to do more with his life, so he resigned and proceeded to enlist with the Texas National Guard. This is where he met his hero, Audie Murphy.

As a decorated soldier from World War II, Audie Murphy was known by many and, to Roy's surprise, Audie Murphy was much like him – short in height and coming from a not well-off family background. He learned so much from his time in the National Guard, joining in during the Korean War.

With his combined teachings from family, mentors and hero, Roy wanted to do more once again. He gave this next tribute for his loved one. He then made his next move to enlist in the regular army when he was only nineteen years old.

TRAINING FOR THE WAR:

Roy received training like all other enlistees in the MP. As soon as he graduated, he was deployed to Vietnam with the 82nd Airborne Division from 1959 to 1965. There, he met an Australian Warrant Officer named Dickey who had just come from a mission in a Malaysian Jungle, battling Communists. Unbeknownst to Roy, Dickey would be another sort of mentor to him, teaching him the importance of blending in, so Roy learned the ways of the Vietnamese people, from how they walked and how they ate.

In 1966, Roy stepped on a landmine and was sent to the Clark Air Force Base in the Philippines, where he was told he was paralyzed from the waist down. Then, he was brought to Fort Sam Houston in Texas, and he was told that his injuries were too severe, and he might never walk again. However, if there is one thing that has been learned about Roy is that he is a fighter. He fought those kids calling him racial slurs, so it seemed that him fighting his own medical condition would not be the most bizarre thing he would do. Every night, he would crawl out of bed and make efforts to walk. Eventually, through sheer determination and hard work, Roy walked out of the hospital.

Roy then requested to be transferred back to the 82nd at Fort Bragg, NC, where he resubmitted his papers to join the Special Forces division. He encountered training like no other in this division of the Army. His physical prowess was tested everyday through harsh obstacle courses with extra double-digit pounds of equipment on him. He was also tested in his intelligence, and specialized in becoming a weapon expert. Like in everything he did, he worked hard and with dedication. And soon enough, his efforts paid off in the way he deserved.

By 1967, he had completed his training with the Special Forces and received to be part of the 5th Special Forces Group. With this team he was deployed back to Vietnam, where he made himself known as a hero of the Vietnam War to the American People.

BATTLE FOUGHT:

On May 2, 1968, Roy was attending Catholic Mass when he heard a distress call over his radio. From the message, he learned that there was a twelve-man team (three Special Forces Soldiers and nine Vietnamese Montagnards, or Mountain Men) in need of rescuing. They were being attacked by the North Vietnamese Army (NVA) Battalion, and they were drastically outnumbered, almost 100 to 1. There were already three attempts for an air rescue; however, they all failed. With no hesitation, Roy grabbed what he could and jumped into the next rescue helicopter.

Unfortunately, the helicopter Roy was on was, as the previous attempts made clear, unable to land or go anywhere near the twelve men in need. So, they landed in a place far from the origin point and went on foot from there. Roy described this moment in his life as "six hours in hell" because of the 75-yard trek he had to go through. This was no mere distance, more so because it was riddled with people firing at him.

By the time he reached the team, he had a gunshot wound in the leg and shrapnel marks on his face. Despite his injuries, he managed to rally the remaining forces, cared for the wounded, and made sure he had his own weapon to defend himself and his fellow men. He then made a way for the rescue helicopter to land and get the twelve-man team to safety. During this time, he was shot in the stomach and was hit again with shrapnel, only this time in his back. In total, he sustained 37 wounds from this battle.

"Six hours" was the number because it took him six hours to save everyone; however, people thought he was dead after all that had happened. He could feel himself being placed in a body bag and he could not move to signal that he was still alive. As one last attempt to show that he was still alive, he spat in the doctor's face. This attempt made the doctor realize he was alive, and soon enough, sent him to the hospital instead.

In the end, even if he was wounded, he was able to save eight out of the twelve men. His injuries needed several different hospitals and over a year to heal. His courage is what people should aspire to have, and his willingness to save his fellowmen has been shared with other people, as it should be.

POST-WAR:

Roy retired from the Army in 1976, and his heroism did not go unrewarded. On February 24, 1981, Roy Benavidez was awarded the Medal of Honor. As President Ronald Reagan said during this ceremony, "If the story of his heroism were a movie script, you would not believe it." This statement from the then-President may be comical in nature, but it is true. Courage such as what Roy displayed during his second tour in Vietnam is nothing short of spectacular.

Testifying in court about his experiences during the Vietnam War, he pleaded for the restoration of benefits to disabled veterans. With his story, it was enough to convince the Congress to bring back social security benefits for the veterans of the United States.

During his days after his service, Roy turned his attention to mentoring and speaking to the American youth. He taught them what he learned from his life, both before and after the war: small choices, no matter whether they are positive or negative, will have an impact on your life and everyone else's.

Since he was focusing on the youth, he also urged them to continue their schooling, despite not finishing school himself. He also encouraged impoverished children to put their street skills to better use by joining the military, instead of joining illegitimate gangs. This thought came from something he said, "I'm proud to be an American, and I'm proud to be a Mexican-American, and I'm proud to be a Catholic and a Christian… I don't want any young kid to ever be ashamed of their heritage."

An elementary school was built in his name in Houston, Texas. Also, a Special Forces Training Facility was named after him as well. And lastly, a military command ship was named after him, "USNS Benavidez".

Roy Benavidez passed away in the year of 1998. His story is just proof that people are capable of such bravery and such selflessness. His life is a testament that determination and willpower, and a reminder that you can do whatever you want as long as you have the actual want, the actual drive to attain it.

Master Sergeant Roy P. Benavidez, a Green Beret soldier who saved lives and his own, through the power of determination.

2

NAVAL AVIATOR TURNED PRISONER OF WAR

ADMIRAL JAMES B. STOCKDALE, THE SYMBOL OF RESISTANCE

BEFORE ENTERING THE WAR:

James B. Stockdale was born in Illinois in December of 1923. He excelled in multiple sports such as football, basketball, and track. He also competed in regional piano competitions; not to mention he graduated second in his High School class. Even though he had multiple achievements in school and his extra-curriculars, he was brought to the Naval Academy during World War II. He graduated there in 1946 and was sent to Pensacola for flight training.

Besides taking flight training, he also earned a master's degree in International Relations from Stanford University, an esteemed university in America. But this was merely one part of his education. He also focused his training as a fighter pilot. After Stanford, he continued to be part of the military.

With determination, he flew almost every propeller-driven aircraft in the Navy's Inventory, but this left him with a desire to do something greater. He applied for Test Pilot School at Patuxen River, Maryland. There, he stood out because of his enthusiasm. He accumulated more than a thousand hours in the F-8U Crusader and he graduated with offers. He was so talented, dedicated and hard working that by the mid 60s, he became a commander of a Navy Fighter Squadron.

There was an incident at the Gulf of Tonkin back in 1964 when the North Vietnamese attacked the U.S Naval vessels. The Gulf of Tonkin was a complex naval event that occurred over two days. According to the U.S Congress, it was an event where two unprecedented attacks from the North Vietnamese torpedo boat, which directed their fire towards the U.S Destroyers Maddox and Turner Joy.

The only reason why Stockdale's squadron was part of this event was because the Johnson Administration thought the events were enough to invoke an American military response. Which makes sense, with the North Vietnamese attacking their Destroyers. Before Stockdale knew it, his country, North Vietnam and himself were at war. Without him knowing, this whole event would change the course of his life, and he would now be known around the world as a Naval Aviator turned Prisoner of War, and survived it.

TRAINING FOR THE WAR:

By the end of the summer of 1965, Stockdale managed to fly into 200 combat missions so far in his career. When he was on his 3rd tour of duty, he was commanding the Carrier Air Group 16 over North Vietnam. He was already on his fly back when his A-4 Skyhawk was shot down from the sky. He ejected and landed in a small village, where he was captured.

Stockdale did not land unharmed. He got several broken bones and was immediately brought to a camp in Hanoi, known as Hanoi Hilton. This camp was infamously known for its brutality. This was the start of Stockdale's journey of being a Prisoner of War in Vietnam, despite him having the highest-ranking in the Naval Officers.

In this camp, he spent several years imprisoned. He was kept under the assumptions that he was the leader of the American resistance against the North Vietnamese. They attempted to use these same American prisoners for Propaganda purposes. Stockdale was physically tortured more than 15 times during his imprisonment. Part of the torture methods were beatings, whippings, and choking with ropes. He was also tortured mentally by being put in a pitch-black room by himself for four years. He was chained with leg irons while this was happening. He was also denied medical care, leading to his malnourishment.

For each year, his jailers kept intensifying the torture level, but Stockdale kept his resolve and continued fighting back.

Stockdale wished to help out the other prisoners; he developed a complete set of rules governing prisoner behavior. With this set of rules, all the other prisoners felt a tinge of hope and empowerment. Many claimed that the rules were based on the stoic philosophy, specifically Epictetus' the Enchiridion. These rules were shared with every other prisoner by word of mouth. This also helped the prisoners protect themselves as much as possible against the attempts of the jailers in using them as propaganda.

That is why he quickly became the leader and also an inspiration for all the Prisoners of War in Hanoi Hilton.

BATTLE FOUGHT:

The peak of the struggle between the American POWs (prisoners of war) and their jailers fell in the spring of 1969. Stockdale was told he would be brought to the foreign journalists where he would be exploited – or rather, "paraded". The term used was being brought "downtown".

Because he would rather hurt himself than carry out their propaganda, he scalped himself with a razor and used a wooden stool to disfigure his face. He knew that his captors would never bring a beaten-up prisoner to the media because it would show that they were being mistreated.

When he discovered that prisoners were dying due to their torture methods, Stockdale slit his wrists to show, again, that he would rather die than submit to what they wanted him to do. His actions were so undeniably extremist that the Communists stopped all forms of torture on him and decided to make peace negotiations instead. They were making deals, a different choice than submitting to their propaganda efforts.

Due to this attempt, the lives of the imprisoned Americans got better. It was not Stockdale's actions that pushed for this new treatment; the death of Ho Chi Minh and the negative publicity for the National League of Families of American Prisoners and Missing in Southeast Asia, H. Ross Perot, and Seaman Doug Hegdahl. All of these actions pushed for the Nixon Administration to demand all POWs to be treated humanely in accordance with the 1954 Geneva Accords.

Note that Stockdale may have been fighting a battle from the inside all the while his wife was fighting for respectful treatment of POW families by being the founder of the League of Families. Because of this, Sybil Stockdale was given the U.S Navy Department's Distinguished Public Service Award by the Chief of Naval Operations. She is the only known wife of an officer to have been awarded such an honor.

Finally, in 1973, Stockdale was released from prison during Operation Homecoming. He was also awarded the Medal of Honor by President Gerald Ford in 1976 due to his heroism and inspirational leadership. This honor was also given to him together with two Distinguished Flying Crosses, three Distinguished Service Medals, four Silver Stars and two Purple Hearts.

POST-WAR:

Stockdale described that the only reason he survived his experiences in the Hanoi Hilton was because of the way he was raised. From his mom's local drama productions where spontaneity and timing were encouraged to his training as an athlete that helped him learn how to endure physical pain, he believed that his whole life prepared him for what he endured.

He served as the president of Naval War College for some time, but retired in 1978. After that, he went on to have an academic career that included being a senior research fellow at Stanford University's Hoover Institution for 15 years. He, along with his wife, co-wrote a book entitled "In Love and War", which described his and his wife's experiences during the Vietnam War.

Accordingly, he wrote numerous articles concerning his Vietnam experience. Such titles include "Ten Years of Reflection and Thoughts of a Philosophical Fighter Pilot". He continued his academic career, was awarded with 11 honorary doctoral degrees, and gave lectures on the Stoicism of Epictetus.

With the request of H. Ross Perot, he became the vice-presidential candidate for the Reform Party in 1992. He retired in 1979, but not without the Secretary of the Navy establishing an award in his honor for being an inspirational leader.

Admiral James Bond Stockdale, along with his wife, lived their lives in Coronado Island. He passed away at the age of 81, on July 5, 2005, due to Alzheimer's disease. To honor him even more, the U.S Navy named its new missile destroyer as the USS Stockdale.

He was truly an inspirational leader, who was the sum of his life experiences and used them to his advantage. Stockdale was indeed a hero of the Vietnam War because he did not let anyone bring him down, not even when he was being tortured. His resolve stayed solid, and he was the epitome of resistance. Stockdale was more than just a military person, more than just a hero. He was someone who inspired the masses and gave them hope that they could also go back home.

3

THE AFRICAN AMERICAN MEDIC HERO

SPECIALIST FIFTH CLASS LAWRENCE JOEL,
OPERATION HUMP SURVIVOR

BEFORE ENTERING THE WAR:

This next soldier is an African-American who was given a hard time due to his skin color. However, as the article continues, it will be seen that the color of his skin does not stop him from wanting to help others, to serve his country. What he was handed in his childhood may have been a heavy aspect of life that most people would be affected negatively, but he was motivated to do greater things; to go on doing amazing actions.

This soldier is Lawrence Joel who was born on February 22, 1928, in Winston-Salem, North Carolina. He is an African-American whose problems did not just come from the color of his skin. His early years of life were spent in poverty. Since the Great Depression happened during his time, it took a big toll on his family causing his separation from his parents six years later. He was raised by foster parents after that event.

Joel graduated from high school in 1945. Afterwards, he joined the Merchant Marine, then enlisted in the Army a year later. He spent his first tour in Postwar Italy. Once he was discharged from his first tour, he wished to become a beautician. However, seeing as the opportunities were limited, he went back to the Army in 1953. During an interview with Time Magazine in 1967, Joel mentioned that it would be hard to make it in America for people with the same color of skin as he did. So, he became an army medic; not as a runner-up, but something that suited his want to help others.

Something that should also be noted is that he served his time during the Korean War which happened from 1950 – 1953. He was an army medic during this time. When he came back, he had already made himself known as a good Army Medic. However, his time in the military was not over because a new war was brewing.

When Joel was 36 years old, he was already a specialist 5 and was assigned to the 1st Battalion in the 503rd Infantry Regiment, 173rd Airborne Brigade. In this position, he was sent to the Vietnam War.

TRAINING FOR THE WAR:

No soldier becomes a hero by sitting in the sidelines. No soldier becomes a hero by not taking action during their defining battle. To truly understand the heroic actions of Lawrence Joel, one must understand the battle that he was in, the battle that named him – that DEFINED him - a hero. This battle was called Operation HUMP. The title comes from the fact that the paratroopers who were going downhill from the base crossed a hump. Hence, the name was created.

It was a search and destroy operation. The Americans and the Australian Forces are the ones who initiated this operation back on November 5, 1965. They involved the U.S 1st Battalion, 503rs Infantry Regiment, 173rd Airborne Brigade and the 1st Battalion of the Royal Australian Regiment.

Operation HUMP's main objective was to drive out the Vietcong, a communist guerilla force, who had taken places on the hills of War Zone D, which is 17.5 miles north of Bien Hoa. The plan was that all American Groups would be coming from the Northwest of the Dong Nai River and Song Be River through a helicopter assault. While the Australia group would be deployed from the south of the Dong Nai.

Basically, the plan was to take back the hills on the War Zone D, search for the people who had taken over the place and destroy all enemy lines. This was the plan that everyone thought thoroughly.

The operation's go signal came on November 8, 1965. The plan, as many things in war, did not go as planned. Almost all sides were ambushed and there were significant casualties on both sides. There were about 49 Americans who were killed and plenty were wounded. There were 2 Australians killed in action as well.

As their plan was going down in flames, they ordered a full evacuation on November 9. This means the battle was nearly 24 hours long and it was named the bloodiest battle of the 173rd Airborne Brigade's history.

BATTLE FOUGHT:

The bloodiest battle the 173rd Airborne Brigade had ever fought was while he was in Operation HUMP, his unit, as most were, ambushed by a Viet Cong force. During this intense battle many things transpired.

Despite being severely wounded, Joel continued his duty as an army medic, treating all the wounded soldiers he could. He also refused to join the medical evacuation and wanted to continue treating on the war field. He was basically injured by machine gun fire twice. But he just "shrugged it off", bandaging himself and kept on tending to the wounded.

Because he kept treating the wounded, he eventually ran out of medical supplies. However, Joel was just as cunning as he was brave, so he improvised splints with bamboo. Joel treated a total of 13 wounded men under the enemy fire. Only when he was completely forced to leave the battlefield did he leave the war zone. According to the Black History Spotlight Article, "His meticulous attention to duty saved a large number of lives, and his unselfish, daring example under most adverse conditions was an inspiration to all." (Lawrence Joel – Love Acceptance and Forgiveness Ministry)

His fierce determination to save as many people as he could, despite his own wounds, was what made him known as a Vietnam War hero. It paved the way for President Lydon B. Johnson to award him with the Congressional Medal of Honor on March 9, 1967. According to President Johnson, "Joel exhibited a very special kind of courage- the unarmed heroism of compassion and service to others." (ASOMF)

Amazingly, he was the first medic to earn the Medal of Honor, the first African American to receive the medal while he was living as well, since the Spanish American War. And to add to the list of him being first, he was the first enlisted man, and first soldier from Winston-Salem to receive the award from the President. He was also awarded a Silver Star.

It truly is a wonderful thing to experience, being the frontrunner for many firsts. He showed that the color of your skin, or where you come from does not matter when it comes to the outcome of your future.

POST-WAR:

He completed 20 years of military service before retiring in 1973. He retired at the rank of Sergeant First Class. He settled back in his hometown in North Carolina where he worked as a counselor in the Veterans Administrations.

Joel also played an active role in the Veterans Affairs and community activities. However, Joel started to have health complications. In 1984, February, Joel died where he was born, Winston-Salem, due to complications from diabetes. He's now buried in Arlington National Cemetery.

Lawrence Joel's story is really a tale of knowing who you are and what you want. At a young age, Joel already knew that he would be part of the military, since he did not even go to college and enlisted as soon as he could. He knew that he wanted to help people so he became an Army Medic. He knew what he wanted, he knew who he was and never wavered. Not even when he was being fired from alll directions.

He stood his ground that day the way he stood his ground throughout his whole life. He helped as many people as he could. Thinking quickly on his feet when needed, he improvised when he ran out of medical supplies. His story is a true statement to what people are capable of if they just stuck to who they are and what they want to achieve. He did not let the color of his skin, or his economic status define who he was. He let his own actions define it. And it made him a hero who would not quit. A hero who would not yield. A hero who would not stop if he could still help.

Lawrence Joel, the Army Medic who saved lives in the bloodiest battle the 173rd Airborne Brigade has ever witnessed, despite being wounded himself. Lawrence Joel, African-American soldier, the first one to be honored since the Spanish-American War. Lawrence Joel, a simple man from Winston-Salem, the first "Simple man" to be honored by the President of the United States. Lawrence Joel, the man who knew who he was, and what he wanted.

4

THE GRUNT PADRE

VINCENT R. CAPODANNO, U.S NAVY CHAPLAIN

BEFORE ENTERING THE WAR:

Interestingly enough, there were clergymen who served during the Vietnam war. One of these men is a famously known hero known as the "Grunt Padre," who served as a medic. However, his story is more than just about healing the injured, but also about the care he showed the Marines, as well as his belief in God.

On February 13, 1929, Vincent Robert Capodanno Jr. was born in Staten Island, New York. He was born to a family of Italian immigrants and was the youngest of ten siblings. Three of his brothers were enlisted in the army when he was in High School, which was during the World War II days.

He was a student at Fordham University, but quickly realized that he had a religious calling for missionary work. He went through religious training at the Maryknolls of the Catholic Foreign Mission Society of America. His parents may have had a hand in his wanting to become part of the clergy. His parents shared with their children the importance of hardwork, family, the strength in pride for your roots, as well as, the great importance of Catholic Faith.

He spent nine years studying theology, academics and basic survival tactics. Once his training was complete, the Archbishop of New York, Francis Cardinal Spellman, led his ordination ceremony in June 1958 before he was sent to Hong Kong and Taiwan to do missionary work. As much as he knew his calling would always have a religious sense, he knew that there was something more he could do. Mainly, he had too much of a difficulty in communication because of the language barrier so, he asked for a transfer to the Navy Chaplain Corp. Then, he was part of the U.S Combat troops who were deployed to Vietnam.

Despite some reluctance from the people around him, he graduated on December 28, 1965 from the U.S Navy Chaplain Corp and was appointed to the Navy Lieutenant position. He saw the need to increase the number of Marine Troops for the battle in Vietnam.

TRAINING FOR THE WAR:

Now known as Lt. Vincent Capodanno ,he was assigned to a Marine combat unit that was deployed to Vietnam due to his prior experience in Asia. Specifically, Capodanno was assigned to the 7th Marine Regiment based near Da Nang. Note that this was not a common occurrence; not a lot of Chaplains decided to go to the front lines of combat units.

Despite Capodanno being a Catholic Priest, he did not let that affect his interactions with people of different faiths. He brought his attention to the "grunts" of the army, meaning the common soldiers. He was often spotted accompanying the marines along their marches or when they went to the field, wanting to be ready to help just in case it was needed. Being a curious and meddlesome fellow, Capodanno would ask the regiment's intelligence officers what was the usual deployment schedule so that he may accompany them. Because of his actions, he got a Bronze Star in 1966.

By 1966 of December, he was then assigned to the 1st Medical Battalion based at the Chu Lai's Field Hospital located in South Vietnam. This was when he started to make a name for himself in the medical war field. He continued to treat the wounded and became a constant companion in that hospital, helping the men in recovery. He founded libraries, coordinated the acceptance and distribution of gifts, and planned outreach programs for the local people near the Chu Lai's Field Hospital Area.

Aside from being designated with the medic role, he also used his spiritual training. He used it to both physically heal the injured men while consoling them through their spiritual needs. He also administered the institution of confessions and gave St. Christopher Medals to people who wanted them. St. Christopher is the patron saint of travelers and is usually given to army men to keep them safe while they are traversing the battlefield.

He even asked for a six-month extension for his tour by 1967. Although he did visit home for a month, he returned to Vietnam right after. He was then assigned to the 1st Battalion of the 5th Marines where their battle was in the Que Son Valley.

BATTLE FOUGHT:

The battle that defined the Grunt Padre's heroism happened on September 4, 1967. This was already his second tour. He was with the 3rd Battalion, 5th Marines when he gave his life in this battle. They requested assistance in the Que Son Valley because they were being attacked by the North Vietnamese Army (NVA) and Viet Cong (VC). A team which included Capodanno, after some reluctance from everyone because they did not know what to feel about a Chaplain going to the front lines, responded to the call.

First, however, Capodanno delivered absolution and communion to the willing Marines before leaving. As the distress call got even more chaotic, Capodanno jumped out of the crater and ran into enemy fire. He first got PFC Stephen Lovejoy to safety. Then he ran back to get Corporal Stephen Connell. When he saw his wounds, he gave him his last rites before pulling him to safety as well. He also ran to get back Sergeant Lawrence Peters. This time, he was struck in the arm with a mortar shrapnel. He again gave the last rites to Peters, keeping him company as he died.

He did this continuously for five more wounded Marines as he was being shot at from all sides. People wanted to help him, but he wanted to help the others first. Finally, he was going to rescue a Corpsman named Armando "Doc" Leal and Corporal Ray Harton. However, when he saw they were both going to get hit, he used his body as a shield. He was struck by the enemy machine gun multiple times.

Once the Marines were able to retrieve his body from the battlefield, they reported that he had his right hand on his chest, eyes closed, and there was a small smile on his face. Even with what he had experienced, he was glad to give his life for his fellowmen, and for his country. He did not just save them physically, but spiritually as well. Even with the enemy firing at them from all directions. And most importantly, he provided comfort to those whose end was near. And that is something truly kind and compassionate, providing comfort in the end despite the circumstances.

POST-WAR:

Capodanno was posthumously awarded the Medal of Honor in January 1969. According to Fordham University's website, the medal was given due to his "conspicuous gallantry and intrepidity at the risk of his life above and beyond the call of duty." He also received a Purple Heart and a Bronze Star, both honors given to those who have fallen during battle.

A memorial was planned in his honor to reveal that they named a ship after him; the USS Capodanno with the motto "Duty with Honor" which everyone believed was a motto Father Capodanno lived by. The ship was also given the Papal Blessing in Naples, but the ship was not the only Military facility named after him. There was the Vincent Robert Capodanno Naval Clinic in Gaeta, Italy; the Capodanno Research Facility at the Navy Personnel Offices in Millington, Tennessee; Staten Island, New York; and Valley Forge, Pennsylvania; there was also the Catholic Chaplains Memorial at Arlington Mall in Washington, SC; and lastly the Chaplain Vincent R. Capodanno Shelter for the Homeless Veterans in Boston, Massachusetts.

This was not the only way they commemorated Padre Grunt. There was an oil painting of him created by Douglas Rosa which is displayed in the Chaplain School in Newport, Rhode Island. This painting shows the last moments of the priest as he struggles to rescue the dying corpsman, also a bronze statue made by Antonio Pierotti that shows the calmness of Father Capodanno can be found in Ft. Wadsworth, Staten Island. And of course, back from his roots, there is a modern sculpture that represents Father Capodanno in Gaeta, Italy.

Military awards have been named in his honor as well, such as the Father Vincent Capodanno Chaplain of the Year Award, which used to be simply Chaplain of the

Year Award. The Knights of Columbus have chosen that Father Capodanno be their patron as well.

Many people gave ways to remember the priest who saved lives not only through medical means but also through emotional and spiritual means which is more than most people ask for, and just what everyone deserves.

5

BEST GENERAL IN THE SOUTH VIETNAMESE ARMY

NGO QUANG TRUONG, VIETNAM'S FINEST COMMANDER

BEFORE ENTERING THE WAR:

Ngo Quang Truong's whole life was dedicated to Vietnam. His toes had been dipped into the military service sector since he was young, despite being born into a wealthy family in December of 1929. Truong was very fortunate to have been given a good education; he graduated from a French Colonial School called My Tho School in 1948 right before the French withdrew from Indochina. Afterwards, Truong enrolled in Thu Duc Military Academy where he trained to be part of the military. By 1954, he graduated with Class 4 and was immediately drafted as an infantry officer in the Vietnamese National Army (VNA).

For twelve years, Truong dedicated himself to parachute training, where he graduated and became commander of 1st Company, 5th Airborne Battalion. After this battalion was eradicated during the battle of Dien Bien Phu in 1954, Truong helped bring it back. Then, in 1955, his team helped eliminate the Binh Xuyen River Pirates. These Pirates were trying to take control of President Ngo Dinh Diem's power over Saigon. Because of his efforts and success, he was promoted to first lieutenant.

During his time as Major and Commander of the 5th Airborne Battalion, he led the air assault into the Do Xa Secret Zone in Minh Long district, Quang Ngai province, and destroyed Viet Cong's B-1 Front Headquarters. While all this was happening, he built a reputation as a Commander who took care of his soldiers at the same time, which seemed to be important, especially since these soldiers put their lives in the hands of their commander. Charisma is not the right word for it, but he should be called a compassionate Commander.

After a year, in 1965, he was still in command of the 5th Airborne Battalion. He then conducted a helicopter assault on Hac Dich Secret Zone in the vicinity of Ong Trinh Mountain in Phuoc Tuy Province (Ba Ria). This was the base area of VC's 7th Division. They fought for two days and they succeeded. This made way for his promotion to Lieutenant colonel and was given the National Defense Medal, Fourth Class.

TRAINING FOR THE WAR:

By 1966, Truong rose in rank in the RVN Airborne Division. He was also transferred to the 1st Division which was based in the Imperial City of Huế. It was not exactly a happy appointment since the RVN was in a civil unrest because of the Diem government's order to kill the Buddhist population.

Truong was a Buddhist himself, but he was still called to command. This whole debacle led him to his first test; the first reason that gave him the right to be named the "Greatest General". In 1968, the city he was guarding was attacked and captured by the NVA. This was back in the Tet Offensive, which left Truong trapped in his headquarters in Mang Ca, Hue Citadel. For the next month, he was in command of the Airborne Troops and the Marines, what became known as the Battle of Hue. Truong eventually led his team to victory, earning him a second star in 1970.

This also served as some sort of homecoming for him because he was then made to command the forces in Viet Cong. This promotion was appointed to him with the personal recommendation of General Creighton Abrams, an American Commander of the Military Assistance Command – Vietnam (MACV), who was simply impressed by Truong's actions; promoting him to Lieutenant General.

With his help, the IV Corps were able to stop the infiltration of the NVA forces coming from the Ho Chi Minh Trail originating from the Cambodian border. He was also able to bring baack the paramilitary Regional Front and Popular Front in the region. Because of his and his team's efforts, the Mekong Delta turned out to be the best secured front in the South Vietnam area.

However, all these experiences Truong faced were merely preparing him for the event that would change his life. He has been in the military since he was young, which meant that he had more than enough experience to prepare him for many events. However, in war, you can never be prepared enough. As great as Truong has proven himself to be, he was no exception to that saying.

BATTLE FOUGHT:

It was with 14 infantry divisions, and 26 separate regiments amounting to over 120,000 troops and 1,200 tanks that the North Vietnamese launch their Easter Offensive back on March 30, 1972. NVA's main goals were to conquer Quang Tri (North), Kontum (Central Highlands) and An Loc (South) which was in Military Region III.

The Easter Offensive began with heavy artillery strikes in the I Corps Area, south of the demilitarized zone. The next wave was on the next day, when the 3 divisions from the North Vietnamese B-5 Front came in to strike the ARVN firebases south of the DMZ, which was guarded by the green ARVN 3rd Division. Sadly, the South Vietnamese were drastically outnumbered, and the North Vietnamese continued to conquer the south.

While each firebase fell, Quang Tri Combat Base was in danger of being conquered as well. Because of the North's power, they did eventually evacuate the base. This erased the ARVN 3rd Division from existence as a division which could have been a fighting chance weapon in this war.

The Communist troops conquered Quang Tri City on May 1, 1972. This was an essential battle because it gave the North control of surrounding provinces. Once this sunk in, President Nguyen Van Thieu relieved Hoang Xuan Lan and replaced him with Truong to command the I Corps. Because Truong already made a reputation for himself as a commander, his arrival was not at all disruptive. His presence actually gave the troops hope.

Assessing the situation first, Truong created a defense plan to hopefully stop the NVA's advances. While this was happening, he created a physical therapy program wherein the soldiers who were severely injured could recover from their injuries and get back to battle, if willing.

In less than a month, the defenses at Hue were stronger than ever, and the units were finally ready to fight again. Truong then created a counteroffensive plan involving three divisions to reconquer the firebases that had been compromised. This would give them extra firepower to help win the war. This was a very intricate plan, which resulted in slow progress, which eventually routed six NVA divisions to retake Quang Tri, Kontum and An Loc.

POST-WAR:

Believe it or not, Truong's story is not all about wins, but also about losses. In 1975, the ARVN defenses in the Central Highlands went down because of the North. The

President ordered Truong to defend Hue. After some time, he was told to retreat, but the order was retracted and then he was ordered to defend Hue to death.

However, he was already starting the retreat and going back cost Truong's forces to suffer. The whole scene turned into a wreck. He was so devastated over losing his beloved ARVN 1st Division that he had a nervous breakdown. When he was finally reunited with his family, they all moved to Falls Church Va. Truong proceeded to write several Historical studies on the Vietnam War for the American Army (U.S Army Center of Military History).

Truong became an American Citizen in 1983 and moved to Springfield, Va where he became a computer Analyst for the Association of American Railroads until 1994. He passed away in Falls Church back in 2007 because of cancer.

He may not have succeeded in all battles, but he is still, to this day, remembered as the greatest commander of the South Vietnamese army. He was a strategic leader dedicated to fight for his own country. General Palmer even mentioned he "deserved a better fate" than the defeat he experienced in the battle of Hue.

Accordingly, he was more than just a leader because he also showed his vulnerability. It shows even the greatest among us can have vulnerable moments. His story showed that no one is perfect, and yet you can still achieve greatness.

He was also humble and selfless. They admired him for his devotion to his work and his loyalty to his fellowmen.

There was no energy of favoritism either. He believed himself a soldier, just like everyone else, and he did not believe in special treatment. He was just happy to have served his country.

PART TWO

HUMANITARIAN HEROES

6

CIVILIAN WARRIOR

COLONEL MAGGIE

BEFORE THE WAR:

Born to the name Margy Reed in Butte Montana in 1916, her stage name was Martha Raye. She used this name for her performances in all mediums: stage, television and the movie screen. As early as three years old, she was exposed to training as a vocalist, dancer and comedian. She was a natural, defining her name both on the Broadway Stage and the billboards of Hollywood by 1930s. Her name blew up in such a way it was up there along with the names of Steve Allen, Charlie Chaplin, Bing Crosby, W.C Fields, Judy Garland, Bob Hope and Rock Hudson.

But she gave that up to pursue a career in military service. She first transferred professions in December 1941, during World War II. Raye became a fledgling of the United Service Organizations (USO). This organization brought other welfare organizations together to give team building services to the U.S Military.

Raye thought of doing more, so she got Kay Francis, Carole Landis, and Mitzi Mayfair to perform on an overseas tour in England and North Africa in October 1942. While there are breaks within the shows, she would help the nurses train in Los Angeles, and aided military medical personnel in field hospitals. When the others left, she carried on by herself, training and performing. But then she got yellow fever and anemia, forcing her to go back to the U.S in March 1943.

However, Raye did not let the fever stop her. After having a taste of helping the nation's service personnel and entertaining them, she wanted to do it again. So, once she recovered, she went back across the seas and spent some time in the Pacific Theater. Then she flew to Germany in 1948 when the Berlin Airlift started. She performed for soldiers and airmen in Germany.

When the Korean War happened in 1950, she and her colleagues visited the United Nations Forces and went to the front lines to give the soldiers some company and entertainment. It did not matter the weather, as long as there were warriors who would fight, she would bring happiness and companionship to them.

HEROISM DURING WAR:

Although the Vietnam War was not the first war Raye had seen, it definitely was the one that set her name as a humanitarian hero. During that war, Raye's involvement with the USO and the entertainment of the Military of

America overseas reached its peak. From 1965 to 1972, Raye spent around four months every year in Vietnam. So approximately, it was no less than eight USO tours. While most of the USO performers stayed in the cities and base camps, Raye went to the frontlines and to the small special forces' camps and isolated outposts around South Vietnam. She would do this because she was also a nurse's aide, lending her helping hand in field hospitals.

Raye spent most of her time with the soldiers, sailors, airmen and marines she met in the front lines and on the military bases. With her constant help, she was given an honorary title of Green Beret by the Fifth Special Forces Group (Airborne). For the marines, they made her an honorary colonel; this is where "Colonel Maggie" came from. She was also dubbed "Maggie of Boondocks".

Her other role was answering letters from military admirers and bringing messages back from the front lines to their families. Even with all she did, she was never paid to be part of the military ranks. She never even did all that for publicity. Her role in the war was completely out of her own volition and will to do something worthwhile with her talents. When asked, Raye said, "enough people are going against the troops. It isn't their fault that they're there. They should be helped."

Despite her work not being for publicity, it did not go unnoticed. She was given a certificate of Appreciation by General William Westmoreland, the commander of Military Assistance Command in Vietnam. He stated that due to her personal desire to be there for these men's comfort away from home, she would be awarded that distinction. In his specific words, he said, "because of your personal desire to present your show for the men at the more remote locations, these men serving under hardship conditions have had the rare pleasure of seeing and talking to a personality who is loved and respected by all and needs an introduction to none."

POST-WAR:

In 1969, Raye became the first woman to receive the Jean Hersholt Humanitarian Award from the Academy of Motion Picture Arts and Sciences. The presenter of this award was Bob Hope who shared that Raye "earned the love, respect and undying admiration of every homesick kid in uniform who so desperately seeks a touch, a feel, a moment of home."

Although the war was over, Raye never let go of the connections she made in the Military waiver. By 1986, the Medals of Maggie campaign was coordinated by the Veterans' Organization. It was a petition for the Congress and the President to give Raye the Presidential Medal of Freedom. This award is meant for civilians, the highest distinction any civilian can be awarded.

However, during the terms of Presidents Ronald Reagan and George H.W. Bush, the petition was unsuccessful. It was only until President Bill Clinton saw the signatures of 40,000 veterans that he approved the petition and awarded

Raye the medal on November 2, 1993. However, due to her medical condition, Roy Benavidez gave her the medal when he went to Bel-Air California. They called her the "Mother Teresa of the Armed Forces".

She was given one more distinction before she passed away. She asked if she could be buried in the Military Cemetery at Fort Bragg, North California, which the military happily granted when she passed away. She was the first civilian woman ever to be given this honor.

Maggie Raye may not have been a military officer by any official means, but her actions proved that she was part of the military family. She gave comfort when it was needed. She even passed messages along from the soldiers to their loved ones back home when she could. She acted, maybe not on the battlefield, but aided the broken spirits of the soldiers and healed them.

She was considered a "comfort medic" if there is such a term. A medic who gave comfort, safety, companionship, and love when they were so far away from home they never thought they could feel these emotions ever again. She was, in every other way, part of the military family.

7

ORPHANAGE IN SAIGON

SISTER MARY LAURENCE

BEFORE THE WAR:

Sister Mary Laurence was originally named Shiela O'Toole in 1929. She was born to Irish immigrant parents and was the eldest of their three children. Sheila inherently loved nature and grew up to be a nature-loving person. Apparently, she was also very sporty—especially good at tennis and basketball. She played sports in both her primary and secondary schools. She even became the sports captain at Sacred Heart College in Hamilton.

As a nature-person, she surely loved animals. As a child, she helped her dad milk their cows and feed other animals. She even had a dog at an early age. Of course, she went to mass every day, even becoming an altar girl. This really shaped her spirituality throughout her life. She was even taught by the mission sisters after her regular school life. All this influenced her desire to become a sister. By 1947, she was brought to the Navitate and by 1950, she made her first profession. Her group was called the Sisters of Our Lady of Missions. Which suited her well enough, as someone who preferred working with her hands better than working from behind a desk.

Despite her training in New Plymouth, Opotiki, Pukekohe, Hulty and Frankton, Hamilton, this woman really had a wish to teach in the ministry. Even her students loved her. She always felt drawn to tools and carpentry, so when she has spare time, she would make furniture pieces such as shelves. She would also make the repairs needed in the Convent.

Her story of becoming a Humanitarian Hero started in 1969 when she volunteered to be on a mission in South Vietnam with her fellow sisters in Thu Duc, Saigon. She was there for six years, working with the Montagnard people who were a tribal group in Vietnam. Feeling inspired, she left her home to work with them more. She lived in Phuoc Long Province to work with the indigenous Montagnard. She built houses with the men of the tribe; using bricks and bamboo they found in the nearby jungle. She also taught the men how to make rattan furniture so they could sell it and make money.

HEROISM DURING WAR:

Sr. Mary Laurence took her final vows in 1956, officially making her a nun of the Sisters of Our Lady of Missions. She took her vows seriously, her responsibility became her life's work.

As the war reached its final stretch, the gunfire and attacks became a daily occurrence. Sr. Mary Laurence kept giving medicine and aiding in the construction of their houses, even if it became an effort to sell during the war. When they were asked to evacuate, she refused because of the Montagnards and by early 1975, they were attacked. She and around 500 refugees fled to the jungle but without proper directions, they wandered around for 10 days not knowing where to go. Sadly, the North Vietnamese Army (NVA) captured them. They were treated poorly in the enemy camp. Interrogations ensued to see if the sisters had anything to do with the CIA but once they were satisfied, they were released from their imprisonment.

Sr. Mary Laurence was then concerned about the 16 children in her order's orphanage, which included the 3 Stieng babies. So, she made sure they had safe passage through an Australian flight out of the country which was referred to as the Operation Babylift. Afterwards, Sr. Mary Laurence found out that her three other sisters were left in Saigon. Against all advice, she went back to get Sr, M. Lea. Sr. Mary Laurence found her three sisters and brought them out through helicopter flights. They left Saigon, and came aboard a cargo ship to the Philippines, where they got a flight to Guam.

Amazingly, there was some downtime when they reached New Zealand. By the end of 1975, Sr. Mary Laurence went to Western Samoa to prepare the land for an agricultural center. When she was done building one with the people, she focused her mind on the practical studies of agriculture such as planting and caring for the farm animals. In other words, for 14 years, she enhanced her rural skills and taught them at the center that was built.

By 1989, Sr. Mary Laurence travelled to Rome. She went to be part of the Congregational Renewal Program. And because she went to Europe, she was given the chance to see her ancestral country, Ireland.

POST-WAR:

After her time in Vietnam, Sr. Mary Laurence did many things. Her work did not stop when the Vietnam War ended. She continued to serve Vietnam despite the war being over. In 1992, she applied to the Volunteer Service Abroad (VSA) scheme so she could teach English in Vietnam. She also went back to her baptismal name, Sheila O'Toole and she taught in Qui Nhon Province for two years. She undoubtedly thought that her mission in Vietnam was not yet over and it soon became obvious that it really was not over.

By 1994, her contract with VSA ended and she took a position in teaching English Night Classes at the Thuc Doc University. As she went back to Vietnam, she was able to reconnect with the people she met during the war. When she received overseas funding, she began a charity for indigenous communities, helping with medicine and housing, improving the lifestyle and health of everyone, especially lepers. She assisted in making a center to help former prostitutes who were out of work in Ho Chi Minh City as well, which later expanded to helping expecting mothers who were cut off from their families.

However, this was not exactly a good mission in the eyes of the authorities. By 2004, Sr. Sheila became the persona non grata and was banished from the country. Which is a painful fate after all she had done for Vietnam. She gave her life for the country and yet she was cast away for the work she did that is not exactly accepted by the masses. When she returned to New Zealand, she started writing memoirs about Vietnam and her works. She also volunteered for the Red Cross, New Zealand Hospice and Meals on Wheels.

In 1986, she was appointed a Companion of the Queen's Service Order for Community Service in Western Samoa. In 2004, she then became a Companion of the New Zealand Order of Merit for her services as a humanitarian. This was a recognition for her work in Vietnam. Sister Shiela O'Toole passed away in June 10, 2024. Thanks to her several nieces and nephews, her memory lives on – her legacy lives on.

8

SOLDIER SCHOLAR

BERNARD FALL, A MILITARY ANALYST

BEFORE THE WAR:

Bernard Fall was born in Vienna in 1926 but was raised and schooled in France. He was even in Riviera when the Germans invaded the place in 1940. His father was a man who served in the army before the fall of France, first a businessman though. His father was also a member of the Underground Resistance.

Bernard then became a member of the Maquis in Savoy and fought in the war with the Germans until they came back to the Southern part of France. For a time, he served in a Moroccan infantry division in the final tours across Europe but he was injured and decorated with the Ordre de la Libération in 1945.

During World War II, Bernard became a researcher for the Nuremberg War Crimes Tribunal and became a student at the University of Paris. Later on, he went to the University of Munich. By late 1950, he got a Fullbright grant to study in the United States where he graduated with a degree of Education from Syracuse University and John Hopkins University. He may not have had an interest in Vietnam in his early years, but when he began to study Indochina and traveled to Southeast Asia in 1953, he took an interest in it.

Finally earning his doctorate from Syracuse in 1966, he then taught at the American University in Washington before leaving for Howard University in 1956. From there, he started to find his interest in Vietnam, with his constant trips to the country. Between teaching in America and going to Vietnam, he would also fund the Rockefeller and Guggenheim Foundations. As his life continued, he became the leading academic critic of the war in Vietnam as well as a committed student of the Indochinese military operations. He was awarded a Certificate of Appreciation in 1961 to thank him for his efforts in securing truthful information.

However, as the war progressed and the Americans became more and more involved, they started to feel uneasy about Bernard Fall. They felt unsure and unsteady about his writings about the Vietnam War which led to a very different turn of events to what he initially thought his life would be.

HEROISM DURING WAR:

The thing about Bernard's writing on the Vietnam War is that it was about academics and analysis of the politics, economics, and security issues of the country during the century. He would also analyze military tactics: what makes a soldier great when it comes to strategy, operational concepts, and tactics. He used a scientist's methodological approach along with relevant related literature.

According to Lewis Bernstein, Bernard was able to capture the significance of warfare in his work. Bernard was also writing with John Shy and Thomas W. Collier, calling their work Revolutionary War. This paper contained the phenomenon of the mid-20th century with its foundation in the theories of Mao Zedong. His research became a book called "Street Without Joy", which is now known as perhaps a military classic. In the book, he narrated the French failure in the first Indochinese War. He had this uncanny ability of being able to blend the details of high-level decision making with the details of operations at the company level.

The book is not just a scientific sort of study but is a book of dramatics as well. The story presents the multiple attempts of the French commanders trying to win the insurgence of Viet Minh. The French had the advantage of Firepower, airpower and mobility. The book ends with the irony of a Greek Tragedy. The French finally got to the battle but, just as the winnings was almost within reach, they lost it.

Bernard wrote more than just a book. He published a doctoral dissertation on the Viet-Minh Regime: Government and Administration in the Democratic

Republic of Vietnam (1954), The Two Vietnams: A Political and Military Analysis (1963), the Vietnam Reader (1965) and many more. His last book was "Hell in a Very Small Place" which is a detailed analysis of the last French attempt to bring Viet Minh to war. His wife, Dorothy Fall, started to write as well, publishing a work in 1967.

Bernard Fall's books lasted for years, until even now. It shows the importance of war analysis and being present during times like these. Its importance still stands firm today.

POST-WAR:

Bernard Fall did not have a life after the Vietnam War. He was killed on February 21, 1967 while he was trying to get more information about Operation Junction City near Hue. He, unfortunately, stepped on a landmine. He died onsite.

However, his memory lives on in his wife, Dorothy Fall, who published "Bernard Fall: Memories of a Soldier-Scholar" in 2006.

9

FOUNDER OF THE SCHOOL OF YOUTH FOR SOCIAL SERVICE

THICH NHAT HANH, AN ON-HANDS BUDDHIST MONK

BEFORE THE WAR:

The story of this Humanitarian hero is one for the books. Thich Nhat Hanh was born in Central Vietnam in 1926. He had a pretty big family in the Ancient Imperial Capital of Hue. His father came from the official land reform in the Imperial Administration under the French. In the birth order, he was second to the last, which is the fifth of his siblings. His family life included his extended family, such as uncles, aunts, cousins, and paternal grandmother.

When Hanh was four, his father was assigned to the northern province of Thanh Hoa; a year after they moved to join him. Even as a kid, Hanh was interested in Buddhism, reading books and magazines his older brother would bring home.

In interviews, Hanh mentioned his pivotal moment when he was nine years old. He was so entranced by a picture of Buddha on the cover of a Nho's Buddhist Magazine. In the illustration, Buddha was sitting on the grass with ease and a smile; it left Hanh with a sense of peace, a big difference from whenever he witnessed the injustice and suffering of the French Colonial rule.

After a year, when he was ten, Hanh and his brothers were talking. His older brother, the same one who brought home Buddhist magazines, said he wanted to be a monk. And he knew, right then, that he wanted to be one as well.

At the age of eleven, Hanh already had his first spiritual experience. He was on a school trip and wandered off, looking for a hermit that was rumored to be there. When he found not the person he was looking for but a well of fresh, pure water. He realized how hot and thirsty he was. When he drank the water, he felt fulfilled and peacefully, as if he found what he was truly looking for.

He started out as a novice monk at the age of 16. They called his rank a young bhikshu. He was actively helping in the movement to bring back Vietnamese Buddhism. He was one of the first young monks to study a secular subject at the University in Saigon.

HEROISM DURING WAR:

Hanh came back to Vietnam in January 1964, entering a leadership role in the Buddhist movement for peace and social action. Meeting with the Buddhist leaders, he proposed that they should dedicate one day every week to spend in the Bamboo Forest Temple for a calm body, mind and soul. The second proposal he made was to invest in the pilot villages for rural reconstruction and development.

Since the Vietnam War was happening around them, he made three more proposals to the Unified Buddhist Congregation to help with the chaos. The first being that the congregation should publicly call for the stop of hostilities in Vietnam and organize negotiations between the North and South. The second proposal was for them to make an institute of Higher Buddhist Studies to train a new generation of Buddhist academics. And the last proposal was that they should make a training center for social workers to help in the rural villages and create social change guided by Buddha's teachings.

When the military seized control of the government in June 1965, chaos became greater than before. Civil liberties were restricted, political opponents—denounced as neutralists or pro-Communists—were imprisoned, and political parties were allowed to operate only if they did not openly criticize government policy. (Thich Nhat Hanh: Extended Biography | Plum Village).

By September 1965, Hanh and his other co-brothers finally created the School of Youth for Social Services (SYSS). This foundation gave a formal structure for the engaged social action that he and his brothers were starting. They made a politically-neutral relief organization to help train people in practical tactics and spiritual power; sending them off to poor villages to help them find new homes or rebuild their agricultural sites.

Hanh furthered his plans in February 1966 by building a community and establishing his Order based on the traditional Buddhist Bodhisattva rules. It symbolized Hanh's teachings of being completely neutral in conflict. He wrote the following: The Vietnam War was, first and foremost, an ideological struggle. To ensure our people's survival, he had to overcome both communist and anticommunist fanaticism, and maintain the strictest neutrality. Buddhists tried their best to speak for all the people and not take sides, but we were condemned as 'pro-communist neutralists.' Both warring parties claimed to speak for what the people really wanted, but the North Vietnamese spoke for the communist bloc and the South Vietnamese spoke for the capitalist bloc. The Buddhists only wanted to create a vehicle for the people to be heard—and the people only wanted peace, not a "victory" by either side. (Thich Nhat Hanh: Extended Biography | Plum Village).

POST-WAR:

His teaching career reached 65 years. His work has revived Buddhism for the 21st century and transformed the religion into a living practice instead of something merely "theoretical". He integrated so many Western ideas into the religion to help it evolve to what it is today giving it more of a universal quality. Some of these western ideas were psychology, science, ecology, ethics, and education.

A month after Hanh's 89th birthday, he was attacked by

a severe brain hemorrhage. This left him paralyzed - unable to speak and walk. The doctors said at first that this was an impossible condition to survive from. However, Hanh did the impossible and recovered. He recovered in France and then in San Francisco.

By 2016, he returned to Plum Village before moving to join the community of young Vietnamese monastics stationed in Thailand. However, even with the treatments, he was still unable to walk and speak. He returned to Vietnam in 2018 to live out the rest of his life at his original temple, the Tu Hieu Temple in Hue. This temple is where he began his Buddhist life, where he became Titular Abbot and Head of lineage over the years. This shows his life came into full circle.

Hanh's legacy lives on in his students who continue what they have learned from him. His teachings of healing, transformation and reconciliation are what give the foundation of the communities of resistance he built around the world. His teachings continue to fill the retreats and training programs of different families, teachers, scientists, social workers, entrepreneurs, ecologists and social activists around the world. Everything he did, he put out in the world continues to grow and move around the earth even though he left this world

Just a final quote from one of the articles of Thich Nhat Hanh. "His aspirations and hopes live on in a thriving community of all ages, nationalities, and backgrounds, continuing to evolve and develop his teachings and practices, making them ever more appropriate to our times" (Thich Nhat Hanh: Extended Biography | Plum Village).

10

RED CROSS VOLUNTEERS

DONUT DOLLIES, RED CROSS VOLUNTEERS WHO PROVIDE
SUPPORT AND COMFORT TO LOCAL COMMUNITIES

BEFORE THE WAR:

The Donut Dollies were 627 constantly upbeat Red Cross women volunteers who served in the Vietnam war. They boosted the soldier's morale through songs, games, or even simple good thoughts. These Donut Dollies actually did not just show up in the Vietnam War but also showed up during World War II. This was when the female Red Cross volunteers went to the soldiers in the field and served coffee and doughnuts. Their nickname of Donut Dollies was also a nod to the Red Cross women who came before them and who did the same thing during the Korean war. Another name for the Donut Dollies was the Supplemental Recreational Activities Overseas (SRAO) program staff.

There were qualifications to become a Donut Dolly. Applicants must be female between 21 to 24 years old, graduated college, and single. They used to go through two weeks of training in Washington, DC to learn the hierarchy and composition of the military, and what to expect in the war zone bases. This is all before they get deployed out of the country.

One of the notable Donut Dollies was Jeanne Christie, who was part of the group when they were in Nha Trang, Dan Nang and Phan Rang in 1967.

The Donut Dollies only travelled by helicopter, truck and/or jeep to reach the military men. However, even if they were not trained to be on the battlefield, they actually saw the consequences of war and experienced different challenges. They were basically the soldier's "support animals" whenever they experienced something truly traumatic, such as seeing death or being injured beyond repair.

In World War I, the United States Government made the American Red Cross give out refreshments at railroad junctions. During World War II, the Red Cross was then put to use in the clubmobile program to give out food, drink and other item needs of the soldiers at that time; giving them some sort of taste of home as they fought. In the Korean War, they went out again doing as they did before.

HEROISM DURING WAR:

The job of the Donut Dollies when they were in Vietnam was to boost up the U.S soldier's morale. They visited almost all-American firebases, bringing board games, records, and treats. Basically, anything to give them comfort and a taste of home. So that, even if they were far away from home, they could still feel the love of their families, and the comfort of being in the safety of their home. Despite what most people would think, they did NOT pass out doughnuts. Despite the Donut Dollies not being part of the military ranks, some still died in the war.

There were testimonies from veterans such as this to Jeanne Christie: "You made us feel less lonely, less abandoned, less cut off from all we hold dear. You made life a little easier for us, took us back home while you were with us and earned our undying gratitude."

These women were young, brave, and bold. They came in the war zones to comfort the soldiers, fully aware of the risks that come with entering any zone that is part of the war. One of the best known Donut Dollies was Pat Rowan who had two tours in Vietnam: one in 1967 – 1968 and another during 1970 – 1971. She said in an interview, "I never felt so appreciated. I never had such fun with other women like that in the close relationships that we developed."

She also mentioned that she saw two very different wars. One was the war that was in the history books, the other was a war within the soldiers' minds themselves. Which war is more terrible is not the correct question, but the war the Donut Dollies fought was the latter, and they did it beautifully.

Sadly, not all military men met a donut dolly, mainly because of the number of men to them. They were merely 600+, compared to how many military men. That is a big number ration. No one appreciated the Donut Dollies' work more than the troops. You may not be able to understand why these women saved the lives of a lot of these men just by their mere presence. They were a reminder of what was waiting for them back home.

POST-WAR:

Seeing as the Donut Dollies were formed during the war, there is not much to say about them post-war. However, most people still remember them for their kindness and comfort. Norm Anderson wrote and directed a movie that showcased the Donut Dollies and what they did during the war. It showed his mother's life as one of the women, her name being Dorset Anderson of Cummington, Massachusetts.

PART THREE

NOTABLE INDIVIDUALS

11

COMMANDER OF THE U.S FORCES IN VIETNAM

WILLIAM WESTMORELAND, THE MILITARY GENIUS

FUN FACT:

Did you know? In pursuit of his strategy of attrition, Westmoreland requested ever more U.S. ground forces. By April 1967, during a trip to Washington, he was seeking to bring the total number of troops up to 550,500, which he called the "minimal essential force," while 670,000 was "the optimum.

BEFORE ENTERING THE WAR:

In Spartanburg, South Carolina, William Westmoreland was born to a family that had roots in the Revolutionary War and served in the Confederate Army during the Civil War. He graduated from West Point in 1936 with the ranking first in Military Leadership. Here, he was actually called "Westly" fondly.

He had some experience before the Vietnam War as he was part of World War II. Westmoreland commanded the artillery units in North Africa and Sicily. He also led the 34th Field Artillery Battalion during the Normandy Invasion. He was chief of staff of the U.S Army's Ninth Division when it entered Germany in 1944.

He also served in the Korean War as the Commander of the 187th Regimental Combat Team. By 1955, Westmoreland was then promoted to Major General. He was ordered to command the 101st Airborne Division in 1958 and became the Superintendent of West Point after two years.

Then, after the Kennedy assassination, the newly appointed President appointed Westmoreland to go to Vietnam as deputy to General Paul Harkins and command the U.S Military Assistance Command in Vietnam. By June 1964, he was a full four-star general and became the Commander of the U.S Forces in Vietnam.

He built a reputation for himself as an organized and disciplined commander, one who gave importance to conventional warfare tactics. He was also known to be formal all the time, and had a set of very strong beliefs in the American Military system. He was not named as Time's Man of the Year at one point for nothing after all.

When Westmoreland arrived in Vietnam in 1964, there were already 16,000 U.S troops in the region. He pushed for the increase of the U.S Military presence in

South Vietnam. He debated if the escalation was needed to prevent the unstable Saigon's government from collapsing because of the Communist North Vietnamese (NVA) and National Liberation Front (NLF) forces, also known as the Viet Cong.

He started the "Search and destroy" operations using airborne vehicles such as helicopters, and high-tech weapons to kill the opposing forces. His strategy was to have faith in the U.S Firepower, such as the intensive aerial bombardments.

REASON OF NOTE:

This man was known for many things. He was known not only for his cool demeanor of reputation but also his command over the role given to him which many deemed amazing. He was the commander of the U.S Military Assistance Command, Vietnam (MACV) from 1964 – 1968, which was the period crucial to the U.S involvement in the Vietnam War. He also developed and implemented the "Search and destroy" operations, which was very controversial, but effective. He also pushed for the "war or attrition" approach, in which the enemy would break because of the firepower the Americans had. Basically, he believed that because the U.S troops had better firepower, the enemy was conceding from fear.

He increased the number of troops when he was in command, from 16,000 in 1964 to 500,000 by 1968.

He was best known for the Tet Offensive which

happened in 1968. This Tet Offensive was a crucial turning point in the war. After the U.S and South Vietnamese forces received a heavy loss (some 90,000 men were killed), Westmoreland was informed that the end of the war was imminent. The Tet Offensive was, sadly, a surprise attack on the South Vietnamese and the U.S armies by the NVA and the Viet Cong during the Lunar New Year. Because of this, Westmoreland knew that the fight was far from over.

Although he was a notable person, his legacy is a bit controversial, because he failed to create strategies for large-unit operations, when he was the one who heralded the crowd to get more people to join the troops. His focus on the body counts and statistics were a bit too intense, and too dependent on.

However, he still did many things in life that gave him the notable position in this article.

POST-WAR:

William Westmoreland's influence was sadly limited to the administration of Richard Nixon. He resigned from the U.S army in 1972, of course first he was the Army's Chief of Staff from 1968 – 1972. He then went back to South Carolina, where he ran as a Republican governor, however he was not successful but he published a memoir, "A Soldier Reports".

In 1982, he sued CBS News for libel over a documentary critical to his leadership. He thought they unknowingly misrepresented the enemy troop's strength when they discussed the Tet Offensive. He filed the lawsuit for 120 million dollars. However, he dropped the lawsuit soon after.

He, as expected, became a noted public supporter of the Vietnam Veterans. He even left the march to the Veteran Memorial in 1982. He passed away in 2005, at the age of 91.

12

BREAKER OF THE PENTAGON PAPERS

NEIL SHEEHAN, A JOURNALIST ON A MISSION

FUN FACT:

Did you know that when Neil Sheehan was a reporter for the New York Times, he was able to get his hands on classified Pentagon Papers of Daniel Ellsberg? He then wrote articles that revealed the secrets of the U.S Department of Defense history about what really happened during the Vietnam War for the Americans.

BEFORE ENTERING THE WAR:

Neil Sheehan was born on October 27, 1936 to Cornelius Mahoney Sheehan. They lived in Holyoke, Massachusetts, where he was raised on their family's dairy farm. Even though he lived the way he did in his early life, it was obvious he dreamt of a life beyond what he was given. Thanks to his mother, who encouraged him to look to the future, he attained scholarships to Mount Hermon

Academy and Harvard. There, he became the editor of Harvard Advocate, a literary magazine organization.

Upon graduating from Harvard, Neil signed up for the U.S Army and he was deployed to Korea. However, after a while, he was then transferred to the 7th Infantry Division newspaper in Tokyo. There he was, editing manuscripts and began to moonlight in the wire service United Press International (UPI) of Tokyo. When the Army discharged him, he became a full-time reporter for the UPI and was stationed in Saigon, where he started to do his work for the Vietnam War.

As the French colonial forces retreated, Vietnam was left divided, with the North under the control of the Communists, led by Ho Chi Minh, who secured crucial support from both the Soviet Union and China. On the other hand, the South was ruled by a regime of weak governments supported by the United States.

Neil was also assigned to Jakarta by the Times. There, he covered the series of events that led to the large-scale massacre of the suspected leftists by the U.S-backed Indonesian Army. Afterwards, he was brought back to write in Vietnam as a Times correspondent. When he was back in Vietnam, he finally found his true purpose.

By the time he got back, the United States was already telling the South Vietnam regime to give the U.S military total control. Neil saw how the Vietnamese people struggled under this war and their struggles with the U.S hovering over them. The VietCong insurgency was increasing so the

U.S resorted to extremist ways to deal with them. This was where he started to become unpopular with the Pentagon and the State Department of the United States.

REASON OF NOTE:

Neil was not someone to shy away from stating facts and his own opinions based on such facts. When he went back to the United States, he was assigned to write about the Pentagon and the White House. The Secretary of Defense Robert McNamara ordered his assistant and other people to compile the documents relating to the relationship between the United States and Vietnam during the war. This compilation of documents ran up to 7,000 pages with 47 volumes. In 1971, Daniel Ellsberg, who was a former State Department employee, grabbed a copy of this document to give to the Senate but they denied seeing it. So, Ellsberg gave the document to Neil Sheehan instead.

Neil read the document, of course. He studied the document, cross referencing it with other accounts. According to Neil's investigation results, he found that the American leaders did not believe in their chances for victory. However, they still continued their involvement because of political reasons - which led to false beliefs.

The Times was about to publish Neil's article with excerpts from the document itself. However, the Nixon administration only then claimed the document top secret and got a court injunction. This meant that the Times was banned from publishing any aspect of the document, or even descriptions of it which caused the Nixon administration to have a battle with the Times that lasted for 15 whole days.

The White House, desperate to win, broke into Ellsberg's psychiatrist office in hopes to find something to show that Ellsberg was an unreliable source, subsequently leading to the Watergate break-in, and causing Nixon's resignation. As the Supreme Court ruled that the First Amendment should be followed, the documents did not have any malintent with national security. So, the Times was allowed to publish. Hence the publication of the Pentagon Papers by the Times turned into a national bestseller.

Neil's discussion on the Vietnam War did not end there. He published another book in 1972 entitled "The Arnheiter Affair" which was about the infamous case of a dangerous commanding officer of the U.S.S. Vance was relieved of his command suddenly.

POST-WAR:

After everything, Neil took a leave from Times. He planned to write a book which he expected to take two to three years. However, he got into an accident. He broke 11 bones and spent 3 months in the hospital. Sadly, this caused him to pause his writing for a year. Despite the financial problems arising after his accident, publishers gave him grants to continue his writing project.

He finally finished his book in 1988 entitled "A Bright

Shining Lie: John Paul Vann and America in Vietnam". This book got comments from its readers praising it as one of the greatest book ever written about that war. Neil said that he wrote like a reporter and a historian, a perfect blend of both to fully relay the events of the Vietnam War.

The book received the 1989 Pulitzer Prize for Nonfiction. In that same year, Neil went back to Vietnam to tour both North and South, interviewing both sides regarding the Vietnam war. He then published a book about the two sides, entitled "After the War Was Over" in 1992.

He also became an early critic of the Iraq war. He wrote one last book called "A Fiery Peace in a Cold War" which told a story of Bernard Schriever, the Air Force General who led the U.S Intercontinental Ballistic Missile Program.

He passed away at his home in Washington at the age of 84 on January 7, 2021.

WORKS CITED

- A49bbe8a_Admin. "Father Capodanno Biography - Archdiocese for the Military, USA." Archdiocese for the Military, USA, 3 Jan. 2024, www.milarch.org/father-capodanno/bio.

- About Lawrence Joel. www.ljvm.com/venue-info/about-lawrence-joel.

- Academy of Achievement. "Admiral James B. Stockdale, USN | Academy of Achievement." Academy of Achievement, 17 Feb. 2022, achievement.org/achiever/admiral-james-b-stockdale.

- ASOMF. "Operation HUMP." ASOMF, 29 Nov. 2022, www.asomf.org/operation-hump.

- ---. "THE STORY OF SPECIALIST FIFTH CLASS LAWRENCE JOEL." ASOMF, 21 Feb. 2024, www.asomf.org/the-story-of-specialist-fifth-class-lawrence-joel.

- Bauer, Patricia. "Gulf of Tonkin Incident (1964) | Definition, Date, Summary, Significance, and Facts." Encyclopedia Britannica, 9 Dec. 2024, www.britannica.com/event/Gulf-of-Tonkin-incident.

- Dnewbold, and James H. Willbanks. "'the Most Brilliant Commander': Ngo Quang Truong."

- HistoryNet, 21 Dec. 2021, www.historynet.com/the-most-brilliant-commander-ngo-quang-truong.

- Fletcher, Zita Ballinger, and Doug Sterner. "How a Severely Wounded Medic Risked His Life to Save Others in Vietnam." HistoryNet, 25 July 2022, www.historynet.com/lawrence-joel-medic-vietnam.

- Fordham University. Vincent R. Capodanno | Fordham. www.fordham.edu/about/leadership-and-administration/administrative-offices/office-of-the-president/about/hall-of-honor/vincent-r-capodanno.

- Gurske, Walter. "Ngô Quang Truong — I Like to Hear Myself Talk History." I Like to Hear Myself Talk History, 12 Apr. 2023, www.hearmyselftalkhistory.com/biographies/ng-quang-trng. Accessed 28 Jan. 2025.

- Lawrence Joel – Love Acceptance and Forgiveness Ministry. 25 June 2024, www.lafministryws.com/lawrence-joel.

- "Medal of Honor Recipient Lawrence Joel." NCDNCR, 8 Nov. 2016, www.dncr.nc.gov/blog/2016/11/08/medal-honor-recipient-lawrence-joel.

- National Museum of the United States Army. www.thenmusa.org/biographies/roy-p-benavidez. Accessed 20 Jan. 2025.

- Page, Jenny. "Vincent R. Capodanno." National Medal of Honor Museum, 22 Aug. 2022, mohmuseum.org/vincent-r-capodanno.

- "Roy Perez Benavidez | Vietnam War | U.S. Army | Medal of Honor Recipient." Congressional Medal of Honor Society, www.cmohs.org/recipients/roy-p-benavidez.

- U.S. Department of Defense. "Medal of Honor Monday: Navy Vice Adm. James Stockdale." U.S. Department of Defense, www.defense.gov/News/Feature-Stories/story/Article/2097870/medal-of-honor-monday-navy-vice-adm-james-stockdale.

- Vice Admiral James B. Stockdale. www.usna.edu/Ethics/bios/index.php.

- Yanez, Andrea. "Meet Courageous Army Master Sergeant Roy Benavidez." National Medal of Honor Museum, 25 Sept. 2024, mohmuseum.org/meet-courageous-army-master-sergeant-roy-benavidez.

- "ABOUT BERNARD FALL." Bernardfall, www.bernard-fall.com/about. Accessed 30 Jan. 2025.

- Admin. "The Donut Dollies of Vietnam." The Army Historical Foundation, 4 June 2021, armyhistory.org/the-donut-dollies-of-vietnam/#:~:text=Female%20Red%20Cross%20workers%20answered,to%20troops%20serving%20in%20Vietnam. Accessed 30 Jan. 2025.

- "Back to a Forgotten Street." National Archives, 16 May 2023, www.archives.gov/publications/prologue/2011/spring/bernard-fall.html. Accessed 30 Jan. 2025.

- 'Donut Dollies' Supported Members of the Military

During Vietnam, Other Wars. www.redcross.org/about-us/news-and-events/news/2021/donut-dollies-supported-us-service-members-during-vietnam-war.html?srsltid=AfmBOoovITb-27jairUjF29VAkUHCaATqwEd6twN4SDT527Tu7uZFmuO. Accessed 30 Jan. 2025.

- Jones, Frank. "BERNARD FALL: FORGOTTEN THEORIST OF WAR (GREAT STRATEGISTS)." War Room - U.S. Army War College, 17 Aug. 2023, warroom.armywarcollege.edu/articles/bernard-fall. Accessed 30 Jan. 2025.

- "'Maggie of the Boondocks': Martha Raye and a Lifetime of Service to the U.S. Armed Forces." National Museum of American History, 8 Nov. 2021, americanhistory.si.edu/explore/stories/maggie-boondocks-martha-raye-and-lifetime-service-us-armed-forces. Accessed 29 Jan. 2025.

- "Remembering Martha Raye WW II, Korea, Vietnam." The American Legion, www.legion.org/information-center/news/your-words/personal-experiences/remembering-martha-raye-ww-ii-korea-vietnam. Accessed 29 Jan. 2025.

- "SISTER SHEILA O'TOOLE (SR MARY LAURENCE) - RNDM." RNDM, 9 Aug. 2024, www.rndm.org/eternal-life/sister-sheila-otoole-sr-mary-laurence.

- Skiba, Katherine. "'Donut Dollies' Served U.S. Troops in Vietnam." AARP, www.aarp.org/home-family/

- voices/veterans/info-2021/donut-dollies-vietnam-war.html. Accessed 30 Jan. 2025.

- "Thich Nhat Hanh: Extended Biography | Plum Village." Plum Village, plumvillage.org/about/thich-nhat-hanh/biography/thich-nhat-hanh-full-biography#peacesocialwork. Accessed 30 Jan. 2025.

- Vietnam Unchronicled: The "Donut Dollies." 24 Feb. 2023, www.moaa.org/micro/vietnam-unchronicled/vietnam-donut. Accessed 30 Jan. 2025.

- "The Waikato Times." The Waikato Times, www.waikatotimes.co.nz/nz-news/350354959/nun-who-launched-wartime-vietnam-rescue-sheila-otoole-rndm-cnzm-qsm-1929-2024.

- History.com Editors. "William Westmoreland." HISTORY, 2 Aug. 2011, www.history.com/topics/vietnam-war/william-westmoreland. Accessed 30 Jan. 2025.

- Sorley, Lewis. "William Westmoreland | Biography, Facts, and Vietnam War." Encyclopedia Britannica, 22 Jan. 2025, www.britannica.com/biography/William-Westmoreland. Accessed 30 Jan. 2025.

- Academy of Achievement. "Neil Sheehan | Academy of Achievement." Academy of Achievement, 9 Feb. 2022, achievement.org/achiever/neil-sheehan. Accessed 3 Feb. 2025.

ABOUT US

moderndaily. PRESS

Modern Daily Press focuses on crafted material especially for kids through subjects that captivate young minds - think action, adventure, and everything that sparks their curiosity!

Our commitment to producing high-quality content reflects our dedication to nurturing the love for reading and learning. Our team of passionate writers, editors, and illustrators work tirelessly to create books that not only entertain but also inspire.

From tales of epic battles to thrilling military adventures, we're on a mission to provide books that have the power to shape young minds.

Click the +Follow button on our Author Page join us as we embark on a journey of exploration and stay updated on our latest releases!

BONUS DOWNLOADS INCLUDED

Download 3 Free Books As Our Bonus Content

What You'll Get:

Scan Here for Bonus Downloads

No Purchase • Instant Access • Safe Download

Printed in Dunstable, United Kingdom